PERTH

Perth is a city that most visitors find a relaxing destination. Its Mediterranean climate, blessed with many sunny days and mostly fine mild winter days, lends itself to a relaxed lifestyle with many outdoor activities seen as one travels through this picturesque city.

People flock to the endless sandy beaches that line Perth's western suburbs. They can be seen twilight sailing on the Swan River or venturing out to Rottnest Island only a short distance from Fremantle.

The city reflects its colonial past, with many old fine buildings still in use to day. They add character set below the huge modern buildings that dominate the skyline.

Western Australia is noted for its spectacular wildflowers, truly one of the wonders of the world when seen in mass in the hills and country areas that lie only a short distance away. One of the finest botanical parks in Australia, in fact in the world, is Kings Park situated high above the city centre. Here the visitor in the spring season and also throughout much of the year, can see some stunning displays of wildflowers.

On the outskirts of Perth are many interesting destinations to visit. It could be the early colonial towns of York, Beverley or Toodyay with their many fine colonial buildings. Just north of Perth, is the unique Benedictine township of New Norcia with informative guided tours around the chapels and art gallery and old school grounds.

You may visit Rottnest Island taking a swim on one of the endless coral lined beaches. The island has no unauthorised motorised vehicles so walking or cycling or taking a bus are the only mode of transport one can take allowing the peaceful, relaxed atmosphere that even the Perth city dwellers adore.

I hope this book shows you how much Perth and Fremantle has to offer the visitor and maybe you'll show others why we live, where we live.

Left: Overlooking the Narrows Bridge towards South Perth.

- The Bankwest Tower, St Georges Terrace.
- The Old Windmill, South Perth.
- The Burswood Hotel.
- Hay Street Mall.

It is a credit to city planners and architects when they can preserve fine older buildings by blending their newly designed structures in harmony with those of the past. It's a win, win scenario for both historians and developers for when we bulldoze down fine old buildings, we loose fine examples of colonial architecture and the passed memories have gone for ever.

BELL TOWER

The Bell Tower is, a beautifully designed structure, the result of a major design competition to house the magnificent 12 bells, from the church of St Martins-in-the-Fields in London.

The bells have been in existence from before the 14th century long before Australia was colonized by Europeans. The bells are a gift to the University of Western Australia, the City of Perth and the people of Western Australia as part of the Bicentennial celebrations held in 1988. The London diocese of the Church of England and the parish of St Martins-in-the-Fields gave their authority to bequeath the bells to Western Australia. A further 5 bells were specially cast for the bicentennial project, one bell each came from the cities of London and Westminster a further three were donated from both Western Australian and British mining companies. Finally a sixth new bell was commissioned by the Western Australian Government to celebrate the second millennium thus creating a final set for the 'ring' of eighteen bells. The older bells have been rung for over 275 years, celebrating the many Royal weddings as far back as 1727 for King George II.

ART GALLERY OF WESTERN AUSTRALIA

The original Art Gallery was founded back in 1895 and originally was part of the Perth Museum. The Art Gallery of Western Australia is particularly noted for its fine collection of indigenous art as well as art and design from Australia and around the world.

GOVERNMENT HOUSE

In 1829, Governor Stirling left his tented accommodation on Garden Island and he came to live at the same grounds that Government House now lies all these years on. It has remained the principal Vice Regal residence since the colony's inception. Ellen, Governor Stirling's wife refused initially to live in the first basic timber cottage preferring to reside in their small country cottage that was built on the banks of the upper Swan River in Guildford. Stirling left the colony he founded in 1835 and the first basic stone building saw four more governors reside there until 1855. The present day building initially took four years to build with Governor Stephen Hampton moving in before completion. The style of the building is what is known as 'Classical Revival' or more specifically known as Fonthill Gothic style, not dissimilar to the architecture found at the Tower of London. It consists of bonded brickwork with square mullioned windows, decorated gables and ogival-capped turrets. The grounds occupy a substantial 3.2 hectares. The original plantings were grown by the famous government botanist James Drummond and are still growing to this day.

Hotel Northbridge: originally called the Royal Standard Hotel built in 1897–1898 from the proceeds of the early gold rush era.

Looking across the early paddocks in the late 1870s towards the original dirt road of Hay Street. This eastern section of Hay Street was actually known as Howick Street but later became a continuation of Hay Street. The Turrets of Government House can be seen on the top far right of the picture.

Perth Early Days

It was the Dutch who were the first to chart the waters of Western Australia. When the Dutch mariner Willem de Vlamingh left the Swan River in 1696 he wrote, "It contained no good country and the coast for hundreds of miles northwards was bare and desolate". How different were the writings of James Stirling in 1827, "The richness of the soils, the bright foliage of the shrubs, the majesty of the surrounding trees, the abrupt and red coloured banks of the river occasionally seen, the view of the blue summits of the mountains from which we were not far distant, made the scenery round the spot as beautiful as anything of the kind I had ever witnessed". His words may well have been embellished as he had long dreamt of establishing a colonial settlement on the banks of the Swan River.

He was later to be granted his wish by the Colonial Office and the small settlement of Perth was founded in 1829. After Captain Fremantle had arrived on the vessel the Challenger to claim the land as a British colony, it was left to Governor Stirling to establish the settlement on the shores of the Swan River. When the first settlers arrived off the vessels the Parmelia and the Sulphur one of the surgeons described as follows: "The vessel that brought them out resembled in some ways, Noah's Ark… if we can imagine the population of one of the parishes of England mixed with sprinkling of half pay officers and some gentlemen from the East and West Indies and a few cockney's, put down on the shores of a wilderness, we shall have some idea of the founders of this interesting colony". Well, it is descendents of these original settlers that are now some of the most established families throughout this state that now live and prosper.

Initially the first settlers were encamped on garden Island or near Fremantle. Many people became impatient, as their first priority would be to settle on their chosen piece of land. Over the next few weeks the Surveyor General John Septmus Roe worked extremely hard subdividing the various parcels of land. There was a fair degree of disquiet as many felt that those close to Stirling got excessive amounts of land as well as being in the best locations, it was not an easy time. Stirling wrote in a despatch to Sir George Murray: "As soon as the difficulty attendant on landing and housing the establishment was surmounted, I caused a exploration of the country immediately in the neighbourhood of the port to be made and the two towns laid out, one, named Fremantle at the entrance to the Swan River and the other Perth about nine miles higher up, on its right or northern bank. Allotments in these towns were speedily occupied by the settlers, who arrived in August and the more diligent among them commenced the erection of temporary buildings".

Boats now were coming in regularly, faster than Stirling would have liked. Between 2 June and 31 December 1829, 18 vessels arrived. For the year 1830, the quantity had increased to 31 vessels arriving bringing the population to over 1700.

Surveyor Roe, had finely surveyed both Fremantle and Perth. The first allotments were allocated to some settlers. Initially, most took leases in Perth, taking their belongings from the coast via the Swan River.

One of the factors that was unforeseen was that many people who had spent most of their funds on purchasing land as well as stock and machinery presumed the soils to be fertile and luxuriant as per the earlier reports in England. They never realized they would have to clear so much and plough back. Most of the these extensive blocks of over 2000 and 3000 acres had only small parcels of land cleared for farming often being only 100 to 200 acres at most. Many relied on credit at the government stores until they had developed their farms. Many of the settlers were inexperienced in farming techniques and it became trial and error to see what would grow where.

Typically, the first temporary accommodation consisted "…of one large tent with a fly, which was divided into three rooms for sleeping, lined with blankets and carpeted with blackboy rushes over which mats were placed, four smaller tents for the employees and one large living tent. Deep trenches were dug around each tent to keep away wild animals or snakes." So, the first formative years had commenced with all their trials and tribulations, it is amazing to look and see a city that has evolved from such frugal beginnings.

THE CLOISTERS

The original Hale Boys School built in 1858 under the directive of Bishop Hale, Perth's first Anglican Bishop, was built by convicts many coming just a short distance from the Barracks at the western end of the Terrace.

It was the first and only secondary school for a few years and attracted the children from the more affluent families. There were 23 pupils in the first year. Over the years many of Perth's leading figures were educated at Bishop Hale's School including the Forrest brothers John who became Premier and Alexander who became Lord Mayor of Perth. In 1971 restoration work was done and later the interiors were gutted to facilitate new offices. Luckily the facade and adjacent fig tree are reminders of its past glory.

ST GEORGES TERRACE

The early photograph is of St Georges Terrace looking west along the dirt road c.1870. On the right are some of the government offices before Barrack Street. Some of the other buildings were private dwellings and one was the home of Dr John Ferguson, the Colonial Surgeon. He arrived on the 'Trusty' December 1842 and was the founder of Houghton Vineyards in the upper Swan.

Perth City Council and other authorities do much to promote the many activities and visual art forms that travellers and residents of Perth can enjoy throughout the year.

PERTH BEACHES

Along the western suburbs of Perth lies a continuous band of sandy beaches on the edge of the vast Indian Ocean. With a climate that Perth enjoys, particularly in the summer, people flock in their hundreds to enjoy the cool breezes that flow over the coast. People surf, windsurf, kite-surf, canoe or simply relax in the warm coastal waters. Do be careful however, Australia has the highest incidence of skin cancer demonstrating how much sun we really do get down under.

Overleaf: Looking across Cottesloe beach at twilight.

LIFE SAVERS

Safety at beaches has always been a major concern for life-savers. In 1908 the first beach patrols were organised and by 1909 the well known Cottesloe Life Saving and Athletic Club, now known as the Cottesloe Surf Life Saving Club was founded. It's a proud organization, having won many life saving events over the years.

Overleaf: Hillarys Boat Harbour

HILLARYS BOAT HARBOUR

Located in the northern coastal suburb of Sorrento are Sorrento Quay and Hillarys Boat Harbour. This is an award winning coastal village style complex. There are protected beaches, restaurants, cafes, shops and hotel accommodation. The complex is particularly noted for the Aquarium of Western Australia and one of its main features is a sophisticated underwater tunnel that is completely transparent allowing you to feel the total affect of being under water and close to the various marine life that normally is difficult to encounter. Nearby those who wish to snorkel can explore the limestone reefs. Here can be found many of the 136 specie of fish where the temperate waters mingle with the tropical waters of the north making it a very important marine environment.

KINGS PARK

One of the most rewarding starts to anyone's first visit to Perth is to drive or walk up to Kings Park via Fraser Avenue. Whether it is day or night, the views of the city are quite magnificent. You can see the layout of the city below that spreads to the edge of the Swan River with the Swan Bell tower and Barrack Street jetty on the edge of the foreshore. Kings Park itself is the largest metropolitan park of any Australian capital city covering 404 hectares.

To the first European settlers, it was known as Mount Eliza named in honour of the wife of the New South Wales Governor Major General Ralph Darling. With the Perth township expanding, 432 acres were set aside in 1872 as a reserve by the Surveyor General Malcolm Fraser. In 1890, another 450 acres were added. On the 1st August 1895 Premier Lord John Forrest planted the foundation tree, a Norfolk Pine (the tree died in 1946 and was replaced). The park was renamed in July 1901 in honour of King Edward VII's accession to the throne after the death of Queen Victoria. The various Kings Park directors and staff have done much to promote the fascinating world of Australian endemic plants. The displays they create each year are a marvel to most visitors particularly in spring.

Top left: To promenade along May Drive was a regular weekend activity for many city folk in the early 1900s. The Avenue of Honour trees were planted for those who lost their lives in the First World War. Initially the roadsides were planted with European Oak but they did not survive so they were replaced with the east coast tree, the Sydney Bangalay (*Eucalyptus bottryoides*). It was a pity that a true Western Australian species could not have been planted.

The nurserymen continually plant or relocate plantings representing all regions of Western Australia. Most are common species but often some of the rare plants are selected from the 13,000 species that are found in this state.

Only a few hours drive from Perth one can visit areas where in season some of the most spectacular wildflower vistas can be viewed where miles upon miles of brightly coloured everlastings litter the hillsides in what we call the 'Mulga Country'.

Quokka

Western Grey Kangaroo

Numbat (*Myrmecobius fasciatus*)

WILDLIFE

The Wildlife of the Perth Region is incredibly rich although, alas with the ever-increasing spread of suburbia, we place increased pressure on our flora and fauna particularly those species that are restricted to the Swan Coastal Plain. Some of our birds and mammals have been pushed back into the hills region. Some like the Numbat, the only fully diurnal marsupial, have retreated to some remnant woodland reserves and only with some dedicated human intervention have these precious animals been saved from an almost certain extinction.

We know that flora of the Perth region alone exceeds 1500 species and over 300 species of birds either reside or migrate through this region. This does not include many of the rare pelagic birds (birds of the high seas) that fly along our coastline. There are nearly 100 species of reptile in the region and the numbers of invertebrates can only be estimated.

The bright flamboyant colours of our parrots are indelibly etched in the memories of many of our visitors who visit this vast state. Our small Fairy-wrens and Robins (opposite) stand out like glistening jewels but one has to look hard for these beautiful creatures away from the urban sprawl.

FREMANTLE

FREMANTLE

Fremantle has a character all of its own. The fine old buildings have been faithfully restored and the markets, cappuccino strip and harbour restaurants offer the visitor a relaxed, inviting atmosphere. There are many reminders of the early colonial days such as the Maritime Museum/Shipwreck Galleries, the Round House, the Maritime Museum and the Fremantle Arts Centre. Set on the mouth of the Swan River, Fremantle is still the major working port for Western Australia moving many millions of tonnes of cargo a year, and the bustle of the harbour sits comfortably with the historic atmosphere and fine buildings. For many visitors, Fremantle is one of the major highlights of their stay in this large State, with so much to see and do.

Left: The Sail and Anchor Hotel
Overleaf: Sunset over the Fremantle Harbour

The Fremantle Street Art Festival is a well co-ordinated event that shows off the talents of not only local street artists but also many overseas artists. Their talents are well loved and they certainly need everyone's support as this is their business and trade and they work so hard at it.

There are also street art painters like Ulla Taylor (left) the Melbourne based artist who for over twenty years has been exhibiting her talents turning boring grey walkways into vibrant colourful canvases.

Above: A local Fremantle lad goes by the name of Cam McAzie, affectionately known as the 'Badpiper'. Well two things, he certainly is not a bad bag piper and the image betrayed belies what a good man he truly is.

FREMANTLE STREET ART FESTIVAL

Fremantle Early Days

Dwellings were erected in Fremantle area before the townsite of Perth was actually established. The small limestone knoll that overlooks the entry to the harbour and the Swan River is where the first building ever built in this state still stand to this day, namely the Round House. It was also the site where the Union Jack was first hoisted for the Proclamation of the state. The date June 17th 1829. Captain Irwin with sailors and marines from the vessel the 'Challenger' and soldiers from the 63rd Regiment read the Proclamation, establishing the colony of Western Australia in the name of King George the Fourth and recognising Captain James Stirling as the new territories acting Lieutenant Governor.

Stirling named the townsite of Fremantle in honour of Captain Fremantle who had done much in the early weeks to assist the newly arrived settlers. Stirling had good reason to honour the man who was later to become one of the most capable Admirals in the British fleet. On the 31st of May, the vessel the Parmelia carrying Stirling and most of the initial settlers was to run aground in Gage Roads. Fremantle lowered his gig from the Challenger and rowed to the Parmelia taking most passengers off the boat and transporting them to Garden Island. He removed as much baggage as possible to lighten the load and luckily in the morning the Parmelia drifted off the sand bank but not before sustaining much damage.

In those first few months of settlement things were very bleak for the settlers in Fremantle and it was to remain difficult times for several years as the coastal town was established. The new arrivals had travelled thousands of miles in cramped vessels, along with pigs, cows and a whole assortment of belongings. They landed in not the most fertile area with hard limestone and sand for much of the ground cover, not knowing what native flora and fauna they could eat. Most were to survive, but it was certainly a test of their fortitude.

It was a bleak situation for the first few years, dysentery was a problem as sewerage systems in the hard limestone rocks left a lot to be desired and there was little fresh water available, unlike the Perth region. John Ewers recorded that George Fletcher Moore described Fremantle in 1832 as 'a bare barren- looking district of sandy coast; the shrubs cut down for firewood, the herbage trodden bare, a few wooden houses, many ragged looking tents… our hotel, a poor public house into which everyone crowded, our colony, a few cheerless dissatisfied people with gloomy looks, plodding their way through the sand from hut to hut to hut to drink grog, and grumble out their discontent.' In contrast, within a few years: 'Now there is a town laid out in regular streets of stone houses…well-kept inns or hotels, in which you can get clean beds and good private rooms.' How the viewpoint changes quickly with time.

Luckily not everyone must have talked so disparagingly or viewed the town in such light, because by the 1860s the population doubled and then in the early 1900s it tripled. Eventually Fremantle became a vibrant part of Western Australia and much loved by many.

High Street showing the Round House at the western end of the street.

The city of Fremantle is said to retain more old colonial buildings still in occupation than any colonial port city in the world. The white and grey building above is a classic example and few people realize that the company occupying this building is the oldest Australian family owned business still running. It was founded by Lionel Samson in 1829. The Samson family is well known to many who know Fremantle's history as not only were the family involved in business but also became mayors of Fremantle. When the brothers Lionel and William stepped ashore off one of the first settler boats the Calista, few would realize what a great influence this family was to have on establishing the City of Fremantle.

FREMANTLE PRISON

It is ironical that from Stirling's dream of having a convict free colony, it was to be become the last penal colony in the British Empire to take prisoners.

Many people do not realise that this state would never have progressed to the degree that it did, if it was not for the 9,688 convicts over 18 years that came to these shores. A prisoner was sent overseas if his term of imprisonment exceeded seven years, in this case to Australia. They were transported after serving at least two years in the home country. Alas, many of them were hardened criminals, which in some ways did not assist the colony.

People may wonder why so much progress was made by prisoners who obviously did not want to be prisoners. Part of the answer lies in the fact that by the mid 1840s, in Britain there was a turning point in the treatment of prisoners and draconian punishments and excessive work loads were no longer common. Also the Pensioner Guards had a better approach to handling convicts. The men also knew that eventual freedom in this country would lead to a possible new life with new lands of their own. The Pensioner Guards that accompanied the prisoners on the ships were retired soldiers and were assigned to guard prisoners for a set period of time. On completion of that period they were given 10 acres of land and their cottage would be built by the convicts.

The first shipment of prisoners was on the ship the Scindian with seventy-five prisoners and guards. The last convict ship was the Hougoumont on 10th January 1868.

Fremantle Prison was designed by Capt. H. Wray and modelled on the English prison Pentonville. The building work commenced in 1851 and was to continue for eight years, which gives some idea of the scale of this project. The project was directed by the Colonial Comptroller General, Mr E. Y. W. Henderson who, incidentally, wanted the prison built on the top of Mt Eliza overlooking Perth. This was flatly rejected by the Legislative Council. Stone was quarried from North Fremantle and timber cut from Woodmans Point.

There was such a need to house the prisoners that when the prison was half built they moved into one end of the building.

Along with the Barracks in Perth, the Fremantle Prison was by far the largest structure built in Perth and until one passes through the entrance gate, the huge dimension of this building cannot be appreciated. It's a visit well worthwhile if you are Interested in Western Australia's past and the hardships that prisoners had to endure.

The prison was still in use until 1993 when prisoners were relocated to Casuarina.

Set in six acres of land the Art Centre is a peaceful retreat for many who wish to escape from the hectic pace of the modern world. Initially one would have no idea of what historical events occurred within these walls. In 1864 it was built and known as the Convict Establishment Fremantle Lunatic Asylum and Invalid Depot.

It took the convict teams nearly three years to build using local limestone and shingles for the roof. The first patients were admitted in 1865. It was recorded that there were thirty-two mentally unfit 'lunatics', comprising of 'colonial' lunatics (local residents), 'imperial lunatics' (convict settlers), and 'criminal lunatics' (prisoners). All had been housed in the stone warehouses of Daniel Scott which was a totally inadequate structure. The principle behind the asylum was based on the British designed asylums where their policy was to 'cure' the 'insane' by housing them in a gentle environment. Well if you have visited the Arts Centre which it is today, you will certainly feel at peace, regardless of its varied past.

The building was designed to house just over 100 patients but in the early 1900s the number was reaching ridiculous levels with 360 patients and there was pressure to have the building condemned. In 1908, patients were moved to Mt Claremont. In 1909 it was reopened for 'aged and impoverished women'. From the 1860s destitute women had been sent to the Perth Poor House in Murray Street, by 1907 there were too many women for the facility to handle and it was decided that the asylum would be an ideal place.

Over the following years it housed various groups until the war years when US naval staff were billeted there. At the end of the war the Education Department used the building. Again in 1957, it was recommended that it be demolished but it was saved partly by the efforts of Mayor Sir Frederick Samson. The voting numbers for and against the demolition were very close but Mr Samson had the deciding vote. In 1958 Samson proposed that the building be restored as a museum and arts centre in conjunction with the State Government and Fremantle Council. This was rejected at the time, however, in 1965 the State Government agreed to contribute to the restoration and in October 1970, it became the Fremantle History Museum and nowadays the Fremantle Art Centre. We have to thank the foresight of Frederick Samson for saving what would be another lost West Australian treasure from the past. Today it exhibits wonderful art shows, gives various classes in the arts, holds music festivals, sells art ware and has a most inviting small cafeteria set in the grounds.

FREMANTLE ARTS CENTRE

The markets have been in operation for over 100 years. The foundation stone for the site of the Fremantle Markets was laid by the State's first Premier, Sir John Forrest, in 1897. They are a popular attraction both for international visitors and for the people of Perth selling not only fresh produce but also a wide range of clothing, homeware and gifts.

ARTHURS HEAD

The young 28 year old Captain Charles Fremantle, a man mature beyond his years, had arrived on the ship the Challenger. He anchored off Garden Island on the 25th April 1829. He wrote of one of his first tasks, '...formal possession was taken of the whole of the West Coast of New Holland in the name of his Britannic Majesty and the Union Jack was hoisted on the South Head of the River.'

The South Head he mentions was Arthur's Head, named by Stirling in honour of Governor Arthur of Van Diemans Land (Tasmania) as thanks for hosting Stirling when he was in those waters.

The photograph is one of the first to be taken of Arthurs Head. It shows the oldest colonial building remaining in Perth, the Round House built 1830 to 1831, not truly a round house as it has 12 sides.

The Round House was designed as a prison and was soon put to use; at one stage it housed 45 prisoners, a ridiculous situation for an 8 cell prison. Luckily that was to change when the huge Fremantle Prison was built between 1851 and 1859. The notorious Mr Henry Vincent was the prison warder at the Round House before he left to be senior warder on Rottnest Island as the poor Nyoongar prisoners were soon to find out. It was also the site for the first hanging in Western Australia in 1844.

From 1865, the Round House held indigenous prisoners until they were transported to Rottnest. The other buildings in the photograph have all been demolished.

FREMANTLE HARBOUR

Over the years the harbour has seen warships, ships carrying newly arrived emigrants and countless forms of import and export goods. One such export was that of sandalwood.

Sandalwood has been used in East Asia, particularly China, for centuries. Its aromatic fragrance used in thousands of temples throughout the East. The Chinese ground the sandalwood into powder and mixed it with clay to make joss sticks. Before the Australian bush gave up its wealth of Sandalwood, most of the supplies came from India, Timor and the Hawaiian islands. Like the Christmas tree, Sandalwood is a parasitic plant and needs other plants nearby to feed off. It is one of the slowest growing trees, taking as long as 100 years to have a 6 inch (150 mm) diameter trunk. Sandalwood helped many who had no trades and little money as all they needed was a horse, a strong cart and axe. Sandalwood 'pullers' as they were called, travelled throughout the state. Initially sandalwood was gathered by the early settlers, who had to clear their land. It gave them a useful income when they were struggling to get farms up and running. The first shipment of 4 tons of sandalwood left for the Far East in 1845. They got such a good price that the word soon spread and the industry began in earnest. In 1848, 1,335 tons were exported, equaling 45% of the colony's exports.

Windjammers opposite:

Windjammers were a large sailing ship with an iron-steel hull. They looked so impressive with their three or four main masts and several square sails to each mast.

They were cheaper than wooden hulled ships and took up less space which allowed for greater cargo as well as being considerably longer than their timber counterparts and incredibly fast ships. They were built primarily between the 1870s and 1900 before the steamships were introduced.

This magnificent building was opened in 2002. The architects Cox Howlett and Bailey Woodland were inspired by some of the early sailing vessels of Fremantle. The roof structures emulate the upturned hulls of early sailing boats. The Maritime Museum houses a host of sea related vessels and memorabilia from vast submarines to the famous Australia II racing yacht that was the first non-American boat to win the Americas Cup. The building is not only visited by numerous visitors on foot but is also an impressive structure to see for all those people that sail into Fremantle Harbour.

61

ROTTNEST

Even though it's a short journey to Rottnest, its like a million miles away when one escapes to the more remote beaches away from the main settlement. Most people congregate around the main settlement but if you choose to venture further, there are lovely small beach coves some with exceptionally good coral reefs. Many holidayers, take their boats and it has for years been a traditional family holiday location for many Perth families. There are no vehicles allowed on the island save those that are used by the island authorities. Walking or cycling are the only form of travel unless you take the bus which does a round trip of the island.

The Dutch navigator Frederick de Houtman was the first European to sight the island of Rottnest on 19th July 1619. Then in 1658 Samuel Volkersen skipper of the Dutch fluit Waeckende Boey charted the waters around Rottnest stating, 'It is dangerous to land there on account of the reefs or rock alongside the coast.' He was correct on that point but not when he wrote. 'I presume that both fresh water and wood will be found there in abundance.' Some wood yes but fresh water very little. It was Willem de Vlamingh who named the island 'Rottnest', the Dutch for rats nest after the numerous Quokkas on the island.

Before Stirling made his journeys to the colonies another Englishman, well not truly an Englishman as he was born in Sydney, Lieutenant Phillip Parker King captain of the Bathurst landed and explored the island in 1822. The first Europeans to settle on the island with their family were Robert Thompson and his wife Caroline, who had arrived in the colony aboard the Atwick in October 1829.

Nowadays, Rottnest is always associated with holidays and relaxing times and warrants such thoughts but its past is a very sad one for the Nyoongars who were imprisoned there. There was an outbreak of illness amongst the Indigenous prisoners on the mainland and Stirling and others planned for a 'reformatory for savages' and to have the inmates transported to the island. You can imagine what it did to the souls of the Nyoongar people who were free spirited people whose life was centred on free movement throughout the lands. Thompson relinquished his land to the government for of 100 sterling. Soon after, Henry Vincent, a gaoler from Fremantle, was hired to set up an institution for prisoners on the island. He must not have been a caring individual towards the Indigenous people for in 1846 he 'appeared in court for maltreatment to natives.

Opposite page: Little Armstrong Bay Overleaf: City of York Bay

Opposite: Longreach Bay

Above: Relaxing at Hotel Rottnest (formerly the Quokka Arms)

Overleaf: viewing sea life at City of York Bay and 'The Basin'

The ladies dresses have certainly changed with time but some of the old limestone walls and the jetty still remain.

The chapel was built by the prisoners in 1858 under the supervision of Vincent who was superintendent from 1839 till 1866. It was also used as a schoolhouse and a reading library where people would come and read under candle light. There are reminders of the harsher times as seen by the prison grill on a cell door.

The Nyoongar

The Nyoongar people of the South West occupy one of the largest cohesive indigenous regions within Australia. At the time of European settlement, the population was estimated to be fewer than 10,000 people. They shared a common culture and similar language. Within this area there were at least thirteen distinct socio-linguistic groups. The Nyoongar region extended across the entire southwest corner below a line from just north of Geraldton to Esperance on the south coast. The Nyoongar boundary almost follows the natural eucalypt-mulga tree line. The region generally has a moderate climate compared with the desert regions further east and north.

The Swan Coastal Plain has been occupied for hundreds, if not thousands, of years by one of the thirteen linguistic groups known as the Whadjug who spoke Wajuk. The indigenous people north of the Swan River were known as the Mooro and south of the Swan River the region was the territory of the Beeliar people. Those centred on the Swan River were called the Darbalyung people. The land where Perth stands is known as Boorlo and that of Fremantle, Walyalup. The family groups would basically take the same travel routes they had taken for generations. It was not like the European myth of going 'Walkabout'; they followed clearly defined routes that took into account the various seasons and availability of differing foods. Yes, they were nomads but it was a controlled form of travel. There was no need to change these travel paths, as their knowledge of the land was passed down from generation to generation. Failure to adhere to set routes and time of year to travel could lead to major problems for the travelling clan. The territory they walked through was theirs and to attempt to enter other clans' areas without first having consent to enter would lead to retribution. One can imagine how they felt when Europeans invaded their shores, their territory, and the land that had been passed down through generations. There was trading between the various linguistic groups and certain 'totem' foods could not be hunted by individuals. These laws were a method of maintaining a natural balance in food availability, a subtle technique in the preservation of various animals species.

The European spring covers the months September, October and November but this does not totally correspond with the Nyoongar's perception of the seasons. They perceive a far more subtle change in the weather patterns and seasons. They see a year as having six seasons, unlike our four. They see spring covering a period known as 'Djilba', which includes just two months, August and September. August to them is not winter, how can it be, as there is prolific flowering growth both to the north and south of Perth and some birds are starting to breed. No, June and July is their winter. For those who are intimate with the bush, it is an understandable concept. There is obviously overlap of the seasons and flowering periods. What is flowering in the Geraldton region will differ from Walpole not only in response to temperature variance but also to rainfall. The Swan Coastal Plain Nyoongars, the Whadjug, would leave the coastal lands in late autumn, April and May. They called this time 'Djeran'. Often the Swan River would get flooded, fish would not be as plentiful and much of the land would become boggy and difficult to traverse, good for tracking but hard to walk through. Many would not return to the coastal plain until early summer, late Kambarang to the Nyoongar. Knowledge of the weather and the seasons played such a vital role for the indigenous people; for them it was a matter of survival, the seasons and weather was far more relevant to the indigenous peoples compared with our modern times when a flick of the switch turns on the heater, the air conditioner or the water tap. There is, however, this romantic notion that life was simply 'bliss' and everything was in abundance. Most of the time it was but often there would be droughts, heavy rains, illness in the family unit or occasionally tribal conflicts. So it was not always easy, and it was vital to all to have substantial knowledge of the environment in order to survive. They could live where Europeans would die, as Burke and Wills did on Coopers Creek; across the creek; the local indigenous tribe were alive and well while alas, Burke and Wills were slowly dying from starvation.

Sometimes the question is asked, 'Why did the indigenous people not develop items like the wheel or grow crops over the last 10,000 years while they were on this island continent?' Well, maybe there lies part of the answer: 'the island continent.' Cut off from Asia for several thousand years, there was not the influence of cultural ideas from one race to another. The knowledge of growing crops, the wheel, working metals, etc. never came to this land. To change from a 'hunter-gatherer' lifestyle to a sedentary farming environment requires hundreds of years in evolution that just never occurred here. In the northern hemisphere it evolved over thousands of years but by the time it had gained momentum and sophistication, Australia had still not been explored and was not colonised until as late as the mid eighteenth century. The indigenous people were true hunter-gatherers, living in harmony with the environment. They did not try to dominate the land or change it in any drastic way. There was no reason to change. It simply worked. They had the 'law'. They had their spiritual beliefs and knowledge of the land. They knew their skin groups, their totems and where they could and could not go for them, why change?

Much of the land we walk on now has been walked on for thousands of years by the first Australians. Let us at least respect their history and acknowledge their amazing culture, which has existed in harmony with the land for a long, long time.